HEALTHY·LIVING

Talking About

Illnesses

By Hazel Edwards
and Goldie Alexander

Gareth Stevens
Publishing

Please visit our Web site **www.garethstevens.com**. For a free color catalog of all our high-quality books, call toll free 1-800-542-2595 or fax 1-877-542-2596.

Library of Congress Cataloging-in-Publication Data

Edwards, Hazel.
Talking about illnesses / Hazel Edwards and Goldie Alexander.
    p. cm. — (Healthy living)
Includes index.
ISBN 978-1-4339-3657-9 (lib. bdg.)
1. Mediciine—Juvenile literature. 2. Children—Diseases—Juvenile literature. 3. Health—Juvenile literature. I. Alexander, Goldie. II. Title.
R130.5.E39 2010
610—dc22
                              2009043456

Published in 2010 by

Gareth Stevens Publishing

111 East 14th Street, Suite 349

New York, NY 10003

© 2010 Blake Publishing

For Gareth Stevens Publishing:

Art Direction: Haley Harasymiw

Editorial Direction: Kerri O'Donnell

Cover photo: iStockphoto

Photos and illustrations:

Shutterstock.com, page 9; iStockphoto, pages 4–8, 10–17, 19–30; Newspix, page 25; Photos.com, page 6; UC Publishing, pages 4 (top), 15 (top) and 29 (hand).

Printed in the United States of America

CPSIA compliance information: Batch #CW10GS: For further information contact Gareth Stevens, New York, New York, at 1-800-542-2595.

Contents

Common and uncommon illnesses

Sooner or later, everyone gets sick. **Germs**, and the illnesses they bring, are part of life. You might get a common illness such as a cold, **influenza** (flu), upset stomach, sore throat, earache, or conjunctivitis (pink eye). You might develop a rash or fever. With a trip to the doctor, a little medicine, and some time snuggled up in bed, you're soon as good as new. Overcoming sicknesses makes your body tougher so it can defend itself against illness the next time it attacks!

+Emergen
Admissions
Main Entran
All Depts

Some people are born with serious or uncommon illnesses or develop them later in life. Perhaps someone in your family, or a friend, lives with a health condition like **cerebral** palsy, asthma, or epilepsy. Maybe you know someone with diabetes or cancer. It can be hard to understand why these things happen or what they mean. These Web sites all provide information you can trust:

kidshealth.org

www.hhs.gov

www.hhs.gov/kids

www.cdc.gov/family/kidsites/index.htm

www.brainpop.com/health

health.nih.gov

www.who.int/en

children.webmd.com

An old-fashioned way of describing a healthy person is to say they are able-bodied. Their bodies are able to function well. People whose bodies are not able to function in the same way are sometimes described as disabled or impaired. The way they are different is called a **disability** or impairment. Examples of these are blindness, deafness, and Down syndrome.

Did you know that around 20 percent of all Americans live with a disability? Or that almost 90 percent of children with a disability attend a school just like yours? Want to find out more? There's information you can trust at:

www.nichcy.org

www.childwelfare.gov

www.hhs.gov

www.acf.hhs.gov

downsyndrome.com

fcsn.org

school.familyeducation.com

TRAUMA & EMERGENCY UNIT

Not all sick kids stay in a hospital. Many receive **outpatient** treatment. These kids live at home. Some might even go to your school.

Common illnesses

The common cold

Having a cough is a very common problem for children. The most common cause is a respiratory tract **infection** (commonly called a cold). Young children can have 6 to 12 respiratory tract infections per year. These are usually caused by a **virus**.

Cough medicines are not useful in curing these coughs. However, some cough medicines can help soothe a sore throat and, by making you feel a bit sleepy, help you have a better night's sleep. **Antibiotics** don't help with this sort of cough.

You usually don't need to see a doctor if you have a cold. However, you should visit your doctor if you develop a fever, lose your appetite, or have difficulty breathing.

Influenza

Influenza (the flu) is an infection caused by a virus. It affects the nose, throat, lungs, and other parts of the body. In fit and healthy people, the flu is much like a bad cold. Flu **symptoms** may last longer than a cold and you may feel sicker, but almost all people fight off the infection by themselves. Treatment for the flu and a bad cold is much the same. Occasionally, however, the flu can cause serious illness. This depends on the type of virus and your age and general health. The flu can be more serious for elderly or very young people or those who have an underlying chronic disease.

Ear infections

Ear infections are very common in small children. The infections often happen as a result of a virus. It is normal to have some fluid in the middle ear, which usually drains down into the throat. When the tube connecting the middle ear to the throat is blocked, this fluid doesn't drain very well.

Young children get more middle-ear infections than older children do because the tubes connecting the middle ear to the throat are shorter and more horizontal. This makes it easier for germs to reach the middle ear from the nose and throat. These tubes are also softer in younger children and get blocked more easily.

The pressure from the fluid inside the ear can be very painful. Usually, if you have an ear infection, you will also have a **fever**. If you have an ear infection, you should see your doctor. Your doctor may prescribe antibiotics to help clear the infection. However, many cases of middle-ear infection in children clear up on their own after a few days.

Gastroenteritis

Gastroenteritis (stomach flu) is a digestive tract infection that causes diarrhea and vomiting. The vomiting may settle quickly, but the diarrhea can last up to ten days. You might have stomach pains and a fever, and you may not want to eat or drink.

The stomach flu can be caused by many different germs, but viruses and bacteria are the most common causes. In most cases, medicine is not needed.

The main treatment is to keep drinking fluids. This is needed to replace fluid lost through vomiting and diarrhea. It is important for the fluids to be taken even if the diarrhea seems to get worse. Do not take medicines to reduce the vomiting and diarrhea. They do not work and may be harmful.

Stomach flu is **infectious**. People who have it should try to keep away from others until the diarrhea has stopped. If you have stomach flu, you should not go to school, play sports, or visit friends until you are no longer infectious.

One way to help keep germs from spreading is to wash your hands often and well with soap and warm water.

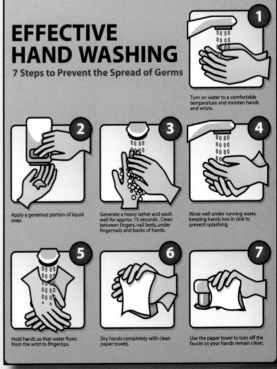

EFFECTIVE HAND WASHING
7 Steps to Prevent the Spread of Germs

1. Turn on water to a comfortable temperature and moisten hands and wrists.

2. Apply a generous portion of liquid soap.

3. Generate a heavy lather and wash well for approx. 15 seconds. Clean between fingers, nail beds, under fingernails and backs of hands.

4. Rinse well under running water, keeping hands low in sink to prevent splashing.

5. Hold hands so that water flows from the wrist to fingertips.

6. Dry hands completely with clean paper towels.

7. Use the paper towel to turn off the faucet so your hands remain clean.

Serious childhood illnesses

Infectious diseases, such as chickenpox, measles, and mumps, can spread very quickly throughout your home, school, and country. While most people recover easily, these diseases can sometimes make people very ill. In extreme cases, they can even cause death. In the past, it was common for children to catch these diseases. Today, most children in the United States are immunized against these diseases.

For centuries, an infectious disease called smallpox affected many people worldwide. It caused a whole-body rash and high fever, and many people died from it. Scientists believe that more than 300 million people died from it in the twentieth century alone. Thanks to widespread **vaccination**, which began in the 1900s, smallpox has become the only human infectious disease to have been completely wiped out. Most countries don't even conduct smallpox vaccinations anymore.

Chickenpox

Chickenpox is an infection caused by a virus. It cannot be treated with antibiotics. It spreads easily, through direct contact with someone who has chickenpox or from inhaling fluid droplets in the air that are a result of a person with chickenpox coughing. The most common signs of chickenpox are fever and a rash. A person with chickenpox is infectious to others from one to two days before the rash develops until the last chickenpox blister has dried up. Children and adults of any age can get chickenpox, but it is more common in children.

By the late 1990s, there were an estimated 30 million measles cases yearly, and nearly 880,000 people died. Eighty-five percent of these deaths occurred in Africa and Southeast Asia.

Measles

Measles is a highly infectious, or contagious, respiratory infection that is caused by a virus. When someone with measles sneezes or coughs, virus droplets are sent through the air and can **infect** others. Symptoms are a rash over the body and flulike symptoms, including a fever, cough, and runny nose.

With measles, symptoms normally go away on their own without medical treatment. A person with measles should be sure to drink plenty of fluids and rest.

Mumps

Mumps is caused by a virus. It's spread when a person breathes in the mumps virus that has been coughed or sneezed into the air by an infectious person. The mumps virus can also spread from person to person by direct contact with infected spit. People with mumps can be infectious up to seven days before and nine days after swelling of the **glands** begins.

Common symptoms of mumps are fever, loss of appetite, tiredness, and headaches. This is followed by swelling and tenderness of the glands within the cheeks, near the jaw, and below the ears. There can be serious effects if you catch mumps after you become a teen.

Immunization

Immunization protects people against serious infections. When a person is vaccinated, their body produces an immune response, similar to what would happen if they were exposed to a disease. But because the exposure is small, the person doesn't suffer any symptoms of the disease. When the immunized person comes in contact with that disease in the future, their immune system will respond fast enough to stop them from developing the disease.

Have you had all your vaccinations?

Vaccination against these diseases is part of routine childhood immunization.

chickenpox   diphtheria   Haemophilus influenzae (type b) (Hib)

hepatitis A   hepatitis B   measles   meningococcal C

mumps   pneumococcal disease   polio   rotavirus

rubella (German measles)   tetanus   whooping cough (pertussis)

9

What is impairment?

Most of us do things like walking, seeing, hearing, speaking, and breathing without thinking about them. We easily complete all sorts of daily tasks—looking after ourselves, learning, and working. But what if we cannot do one or more of those things? Most of us will not be able to perform daily tasks easily at some time in our lives. Sometimes the condition will exist for only a short time. Sometimes it will be lasting. Whether it is brief or lasting, the condition is called an impairment.

Hearing impairment

About three in 3,000 babies are born with a hearing problem. It is the most common form of impairment at birth. Hearing impairment (deafness) can also develop because of certain kinds of injury or illness.

The ear is made of three parts that work together. Sound waves are picked up by the outer ear, then travel through the ear canal to the middle ear. They hit the eardrum and make it **vibrate**. The vibrations then travel to the cochlea in the inner ear. Thousands of tiny hairs in the cochlea send information about the vibrations to a nerve that sends it on to the brain. If the process does not work properly, the ability to hear is impaired.

Go to www.handspeak.com to find out how to talk using American Sign Language—speaking with your hands. That way, your hearing-impaired friends can see what you are saying.

ear canal

eardrum

cochlea

Outer Ear

Middle Ear

Inner Ear

A   B   C   D   E

10

Visual impairment

Our eyes and our brain work together to help us see. If the partnership does not work well, then there is visual impairment such as blindness. When you think of visual impairment, you might imagine complete darkness. However, some visually impaired people can see some light or shadows. Others can't see things clearly. People who have some sight but still need a lot of help are sometimes called legally blind. They cannot perform the same everyday activities as easily as the average person.

People with a visual impairment can do many of the things people without visual impairment do. Just as the average person doesn't think about their eye color every day, people who can't see well don't think about their condition every day. If a blind person asks for help, you should help them. People who use a cane or a guide dog to get around may not need help.

Some blind people use their fingers to read and write. Braille is a form of writing that uses patterns of raised dots.

Learning disabilities

What is a learning disability?

A learning disability means you have problems processing information. You might have trouble listening, thinking, speaking, reading, writing, spelling, or doing math. You might feel confused and keep forgetting things.

These problems are not caused by poor eyesight or hearing, mental retardation, emotional problems, environmental problems, or your cultural or economic background.

12

Jake and trouble go together

There's this boy in my class,
Who goofs around all the time.
He can't listen. Or stay quiet.
He can't read and his writing's a mess.
Jake's always in trouble.

Thick brown hair. Freckles. Funny thumbs.
Button eyes too close together.
Kids call him "Stupid" and "Fatty,"
Sometimes he hits back.
Jake's always in trouble.

His favorite thing is videos.
He knows everything about *Lord of the Rings*.
Everything. He talks a lot.
I won't sit next to him. When I do,
I'm always in trouble.

I am confused, anxious, and frustrated

Children with learning disabilities often feel confused, anxious, and frustrated. They lose trust in themselves. This is because they see themselves doing the wrong thing, making mistakes, and falling behind the other students around them. Imagine trying to make decisions at school if you hear, see, speak, or do things differently than others! It will slow your learning. It takes a lot of effort and intelligence for children with learning disabilities to modify what they see, hear, and touch, and then learn from that. Even then, after doing all that work to learn, they may forget it tomorrow and have to start over again. It is little wonder that children with learning disabilities get frustrated and upset, or want to avoid schoolwork.

What can help?

It is important that children with learning disabilities are supported. They learn best when they feel secure that their efforts will not be made fun of.

Here are some things that you can do to help classmates with learning disabilities:

- Give them praise for effort.
- Give them some direction or hints on how to do a task.
- Make sure they know what instructions the teacher has given.
- Remind them where to go or what to do.
- Remind them of the school rules.
- Be patient with them and do not expect them to be perfect.

Many adults with learning disabilities were unhappy at school. It was where they came to believe they couldn't do anything right. Because of that, they never got a chance to become what they could have. What happens in your school? Are you prepared to help your teacher change someone's future?

Asthma

Dr. Ross answers questions about asthma. Check out what he has to say!

Dr. Ross

Alex: So, just what is asthma?

Dr. Ross: Well, asthma affects your lungs and breathing. The inside of the lung's air passages, called bronchi, become red and swollen, so it's hard for the air to pass in and out. Often, sticky, thick mucus is made, too. This makes the chest feel tight, so you cough and wheeze. You don't feel like that all the time, though. Certain things can set off an attack.

Alex: Who gets asthma?

Dr. Ross: Over 34 million Americans have asthma. Some are born with it, some get asthma when something around them causes it, and some never get it.

Alex: What causes it?

Dr. Ross: Unfortunately, there's no simple answer to that question. Sometimes, asthma is passed on from parents to children. Some people are just sensitive to certain things that cause this reaction in their airways. It might be tiny creatures called dust mites that live in house dust, pollens from plants, or perfumes. It may be pollution, chalk dust, or even mold. Cigarette smoke can cause flare-ups of asthma. Sometimes a cold or flu will cause the airways to become more sensitive than usual. Even a sudden change of weather might do it. The most important thing is to have an asthma action plan.

Alex: What's that?

Dr. Ross: It's instructions written by your doctor to help you, and those around you, cope with your asthma. Having a plan is very important for an asthmatic's safety and well-being.

Check out how Dr. Ross treats most of his asthma patients!

First, we use rescue medications to make it easier to breathe. These are usually inhaled (breathed in) directly. They relieve wheezing, coughing, and shortness of breath.

But their effect wears off quickly. They don't prevent the flare-up from happening in the first place.

An inhaler attached to a spacer ▶

An inhaler and spacer are better than using an inhaler alone, as more medication gets to the lungs where it is needed.

▲ **Using a nebulizer to deliver asthma medication**

Controller medications are used on a regular basis—for example, every morning and night—to control asthma. They work over a long period of time and help heal the airways and prevent asthma symptoms. They may be inhaled or taken as a pill or liquid.

Nine steps to help with an asthma attack

1 Ask if your friend has an inhaler.

2 Give it to them.

3 Sit them down.

4 Remind your friend to sit up straight in order to breathe better.

5 Remind your friend to use the inhaler.

6 Tell an adult if you can.

7 Check how your friend is feeling.

8 Ask if you should send for help.

9 If your friend is OK, you can go and play.

Tip: Don't forget to take a copy of your asthma action plan when you go to a sleepover.

Epilepsy

Have you ever looked at all the connections inside a computer? The brain is even more complicated than that. Epilepsy is a condition that affects the brain.

People with epilepsy have **seizures**. They occur when the messages sent by the brain to the rest of the body suddenly become confused. When this happens, the person may pass out or shake all over.

Most seizures occur without warning, but some people experience a funny feeling in their heads first; they see or hear something unusual. This is called an aura. Some people with epilepsy find that certain things may bring on a seizure, such as playing video games or not getting enough sleep.

Playing video games may bring on a seizure.

What causes epilepsy?

The brain is constantly sending electrical signals to, and receiving signals from, all the parts of the body, as well as taking in messages from the outside world. When too many brain cells send signals at the same time, it creates an overload in the brain. Anything that disturbs the normal pattern of electrical activity in the brain can lead to an epileptic seizure. Some people who have epilepsy might have seizures only once in a while. Others might have them almost every day.

Some possible causes for epilepsy include illness, injury to the brain, or differences in how the brain developed before birth. What causes epilepsy is not known in about three out of every four cases.

What treatment is given to children who have seizures?

Doctors who specialize in the brain and nervous system perform medical tests. One of these may be an EEG test (electroencephalogram). This test measures the electrical activity in the brain. Scans of the brain, such as a CT (computerized tomography) scan or an MRI (magnetic resonance imaging) test, may also be done. All these tests are painless.

Treatment for epilepsy usually involves medication. In some cases, people may need to eat a special diet or even have surgery. The goal is to control seizures so people with epilepsy can live as normally as possible.

What can you do when someone has a seizure?

Don't panic! Most seizures will stop by themselves in less than five minutes.

- Move anything nearby (such as a table or chair) that the person might bang into.

- Ask others to move away.

- Send someone to get help. Teachers are trained to help in these emergencies.

- Put soft things (like pillows or towels) near the person's head to protect it from getting hurt.

- Once the seizure has stopped, roll the person onto his or her side.

- Help the person move to a safe place where he or she can sleep and recover.

- You do not have to hold the person still for safety. Just watch over him or her.

17

Diabetes

Diabetes is a disease that affects how your body uses glucose. Glucose is the sugar that is the body's main source of fuel. Your body needs glucose to keep it running.

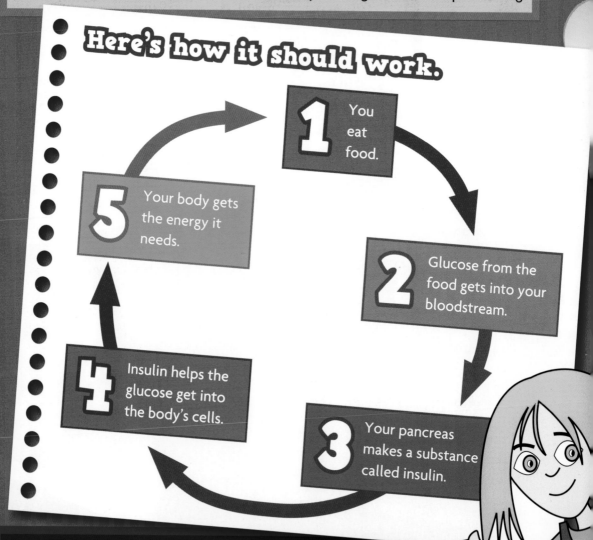

Here's how it should work.

1 You eat food.

2 Glucose from the food gets into your bloodstream.

3 Your pancreas makes a substance called insulin.

4 Insulin helps the glucose get into the body's cells.

5 Your body gets the energy it needs.

The pancreas is a long, flat gland just behind your stomach. It helps your body to **digest** food. It also makes insulin. Insulin opens the doors to the cells of the body. It lets the glucose in. Then the glucose can move out of the blood and into the cells.

If someone has diabetes, either the body can't make insulin or the insulin doesn't work in the body as it should. The glucose can't get into the cells as normal, so the blood sugar level gets too high. Lots of sugar in the blood makes people very sick if they don't get treatment.

Amy's story

When I was seven, Mom noticed that I was drinking more and going to the bathroom more often. I'd wake up thirsty and have to go in the middle of the night.

At my checkup, Doctor Chu made me do a urine test. When the results came back, she said that I probably had diabetes.

Smaller children need someone else to give them an insulin injection.

At the hospital, I had more tests and then the doctors said, "You have Type 1 diabetes. That means your body has stopped making insulin. To fix this, you will have to get insulin through injections. You will also have to test your blood sugar levels several times a day."

Now I get my blood checked and have an insulin injection at breakfast, lunch, dinner, whenever I want a snack, and before I go to bed. I really hate having those shots. It's definitely not fun, but I have to have them to stay healthy.

Apart from testing my blood sugar levels and getting those shots, my days are like everyone else's. The only difference is that I always have to make sure I have my diabetes bag with me. I have to tell someone if I'm feeling dizzy or sick.

My bag is packed with insulin, needles, a blood glucose meter, test strips, and something sugary to eat (in case my blood sugar levels drop really low).

There are five kids at my school with diabetes. The school nurse helps us pay attention to our blood sugar levels and checks our insulin shots.

diabetes
glucose kit

blood
glucose
meter

What causes diabetes?

TYPE 1

Type 1 diabetes occurs when the body does not make insulin at all. Someone with this type has to inject insulin every day. They also have to test their blood—to check that the insulin is working properly and that the amount of sugar in their blood stays normal.

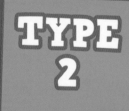

TYPE 2

Type 2 diabetes occurs when the body can't respond to insulin normally. The tendency to get type 2 diabetes is linked to the **genes** a person gets from his or her parents. But eating too many fats and sugars can cause weight gain, which increases a person's risk of developing type 2 diabetes.

More and more people in America have type 2 diabetes. This is because we are eating too many fats and sugars, gaining too much weight, and not exercising enough. You can prevent type 2 diabetes if you balance your food intake and keep up your exercise.

Managing diabetes

Living with diabetes is a three-way balancing act. The medications you take, the food you eat, and the amount of exercise you get all need to work together.

Keeping blood sugar levels close to normal is a challenge. Diabetics must:

- take insulin or pills when recommended
- follow a meal plan
- get regular exercise
- check blood sugar levels often and make changes when necessary

Diabetes can get out of control if diabetics:

- don't take their diabetes medicines as directed
- don't follow their meal plan (such as eating too much or not enough food without adjusting diabetes medicines)
- don't check their blood sugar levels often enough
- have an illness or too much stress
- don't get regular exercise, or exercise more or less than usual without making changes to their diabetes plan

Avoiding junk food and exercising regularly will help prevent the onset of type 2 diabetes.

21

Cancer

Cancer occurs when a type of cell in your body grows in a way that the body can't control. As cancer cells grow, they demand more and more of the body's **nutrition**. Cancer destroys organs and bones, and weakens defenses against other illnesses.

How do you get cancer?

There are many causes of cancer and there are lots of different types.

Some types of cancers are believed to be inherited—that is, the genes you were born with might incline you to certain cancers. For example, if a close relative has had cancer of the breast or the colon, you may be more likely to inherit the tendency to develop those cancers. However, it does not mean that you will.

WARNING! WARNING! WARNING!

There are many things you can do to protect yourself.

- Don't smoke. Cigarettes are known to increase the risk of lung cancer.

- Keep out of the sun. Too much exposure to the sun can increase the risk of skin cancer.

- Eating more vegetables and fruit might help protect you from bowel cancer.

If a doctor suspects that a person has cancer, he or she will order certain tests. Blood cells will be examined under a **microscope**; X-rays or an MRI will be taken to find **tumors**. Often, a small **tissue** sample is examined for cancer cells.

> Just because someone has cancer doesn't mean that he or she will die.

Treating cancers

There are three common methods for treating cancers.

Often, surgeons remove cancerous tissue. Depending on the location of the cancer, **surgery** can be simple or complex. The operation may be an outpatient procedure (where a person is in and out of the hospital on the same day), or it may require the person to stay in the hospital for some time.

Chemotherapy is when the person is given chemicals to treat the cancer. They may experience nausea (wanting to throw up), fatigue (extreme tiredness), hair loss, or other side effects. Some of these side effects happen because the chemotherapy medicines destroy some healthy cells in the process of getting rid of the malignant (bad) cells.

Radiation is another treatment. Radiotherapy machines deliver powerful X-rays or high-energy electrons to the part of a person's body that is affected by cancer. After repeated doses, many cancerous tumors shrink or disappear. Most of the side effects of radiation don't last too long.

scans

September 2009   Volume 83 Number 9   Serving the Protectors

HELP FIGHT CANCER

By John Ballantyne

Despite all the medical advances that have been made in the fight against cancer, the disease remains the second-highest cause of death in the United States. In 2008, more than 565,600 Americans died of cancer. U.S. citizens must continue to fight this deadly disease.

The American Cancer Society (ACS) is a voluntary organization with offices all over the country. They are dedicated to saving the lives of people who have the disease and limiting the suffering they experience, in addition eliminating cancer once and for all. The main efforts of the ACS are focused on research, education, advocacy, and service. You can find out more about the ACS at their Web site: http://www.cancer.org

Have you ever celebrated St. Baldrick's Day? It is the world's largest fundraising event for childhood cancer research. At St. Baldrick's Day events (which happen all over the world many times a year), volunteers shave their heads! Why would they do that? For two reasons. One, as a sign of solidarity for all the children who lose their hair during cancer treatment. And two, to raise awareness and funds to continue the fight against our second-most deadly disease. Would you shave your head for cancer? Consider donating your hair and money to the cause at: http://www.stbaldricks.org

What is cerebral palsy?

"Cerebral" means having to do with the brain. "Palsy" means a weakness or a problem in the way someone moves his or her body.

Someone with cerebral palsy (CP) has trouble controlling the muscles of their body. Some people with CP use wheelchairs, while others need crutches or wear braces. In some cases, a person's speech may be affected or the person might not be able to speak at all.

What causes cerebral palsy?

No one knows for sure what causes CP. Normally, the brain tells the rest of the body exactly what to do and when to do it. When CP affects the brain (depending on what part of the brain is affected), a person might not be able to walk, talk, eat, or play. Someone who can't move like others may still think the same way!

In some cases, injuries to the brain happen before birth or soon after birth.

- CP is the most common childhood physical disability.
- Doctors measure brain injury with high-tech machinery.
- There is no cure for CP—yet!
- Cerebral palsy is not a progressive disease. This means that it does not get worse over time.
- Approximately 500,000 Americans have cerebral palsy.

Managing cerebral palsy

Because cerebral palsy affects each individual differently, there are lots of ways to manage it. A child's doctors, parents, and teachers all work together to develop a treatment plan.

- A physical **therapist** helps maintain a child's body movement and function, if there is injury or illness.

- An occupational therapist helps with handwriting and teaches the child living skills. These skills help the child live well.

- A speech therapist helps with speech problems and/or swallowing.

- Some kids may need to take medicine to help control seizures.

> Just because a kid finds it hard to move or talk like you doesn't mean he or she isn't just as smart.

25

Cystic fibrosis

Mucus, saliva (spit), and bodily fluids all help remove waste from your body. They also protect healthy cells. So, when you are sick, your body increases mucus production to rid your body of the disease. This prevents other cells from getting sick.

To make normal mucus, the body needs a special protein. With cystic fibrosis (CF), this protein is flawed. It produces thick, sticky mucus that causes problems.

For a person who has cystic fibrosis, this thick, sticky mucus can clog up their lungs. This creates a place where bacteria can easily grow—and bacteria cause infections that make you sick. The mucus-producing cells line the digestive tract and make it difficult for people to digest food. This means it is hard to get all the vitamins and nutrients (protein and energy) they need.

Cystic fibrosis interferes with the normal function of certain cells. In particular, it affects the cells that make up:

- the sweat glands in the skin;
- the lining of the passageways inside organs like the lungs, liver, and pancreas, and the digestive and reproductive systems.

Cystic fibrosis can be mild or severe.

In the 1950s, few children with cystic fibrosis lived to attend secondary school. Today, advances in research and medical treatments mean that many people with the disease can now expect to live into their 40s and beyond.

26

What causes cystic fibrosis?

Cystic fibrosis is caused by an inherited gene. This gene tells the unborn baby's cells to produce a flawed or faulty form of a protein called CFTR.

The cells can't regulate the way chloride (an essential chemical) passes from one cell to another. This messes up the essential balance of salt and water that is needed to maintain a normal, thin coating of fluid and mucus inside the organs. That's why the mucus becomes thick and sticky and hard to move.

How is cystic fibrosis treated?

- regular exercise and inhalers
- coughing to help clear lungs
- antibiotics to fight infection
- sometimes a helper gently bangs on the person's chest

Children with CF need lots of calories to help them with their disease. Fats and vitamins quickly leave their bodies, so they need to eat more to make sure they keep enough nutrients in their system.

Things to remember

- There is no cure for cystic fibrosis, but proper treatment can slow down the disease.
- One in 25 people carry the flawed gene, but they will have no symptoms.
- Cystic fibrosis is usually diagnosed at birth.
- You can't catch cystic fibrosis.
- Cystic fibrosis occurs in both boys and girls.

CF kids need your help.

How can I help a sick friend?

Be loving and supportive to the person who is sick.

Be open with the sick person. Don't try to hide your feelings. It's OK to feel upset or angry.

Be cheerful and happy with the person who is sick and with their close friends and relations. You can say how sorry you are that the person is sick, but you don't need to keep saying it.

Being upset and angry with your other friends or family can make them feel uncomfortable. It will not help you or your sick friend.

Sometimes, crying with the family may help all of you.

Keep up the things you like to do—exercise, hang out with friends, and take time for yourself. If you are sad all the time, it won't help anyone. Enjoy your time together with your friend and build good memories.

Encourage your sick friend to do what the doctor has ordered.

Help your friend stay in touch with other friends. This might mean sending letters or emails to school or work, taking schoolwork into school, or lending your friend books or DVDs.

H E L P

Help your friend meditate, exercise, or stick to a special diet by joining in.

Watching DVDs or going to the movies with your friend could be fun. You might go for a walk in the park or maybe just sit on the beach.

Help your friend to do the things they like. Maybe take them out for some pizza at the cafeteria, if they are in the hospital.

Listen to what your friend wants to say and encourage them to talk. Everyone needs to talk. Even if what is being said seems to upset them and you, it is still good to be able to talk to someone who will listen.

FOR SALE

If someone you love is sick

If someone you care about becomes very sick, it can be hard for you, too. Sometimes, it's hard to cope with changes. You still love the person, but you might feel differently about them. You might feel uncomfortable because things are not the same. The amount of time you spend together will probably change. So will the things you do together. But family is always family, and good friends are always friends. Here are some of the feelings you might experience if someone you love is very sick.

You might feel sad and upset. It's OK to feel sad. When someone you love gets sick, life can be strange. Sometimes life is just not fair. Sadness is part of life, too.

You may feel guilty that you are well and running around while they are sick in bed. Feeling guilty will not help the person who is sick. If you are feeling really bad, talk to someone you trust about your feelings.

You may feel scared. Remember, though, that being sick enough to be in a hospital doesn't always mean that the person will die. Most people who are sick get better.

You may feel lost for words. It's hard to know what to say. That's OK. Just be you.

You may feel lonely because you can't be with the person as much as you usually are.

Glossary

antibiotics	substances used to kill some kinds of germs
bacteria	tiny organisms that may cause disease or be helpful
cerebral	having to do with the brain
diagnose	identify an illness from its symptoms and from tests
digest	change the food in the stomach so that the body can use it
disability	particular physical or mental impairment
fever	high body temperature because of an illness
genes	parts of a living cell that control what it looks like and how it grows
germs	small living things that can make you sick
glands	body parts that produce substances to help a body work or to remove harmful matter
immunized	vaccinated to protect against an illness
infect	to give a disease to someone
infection	disease
infectious	able to be passed easily from one person to another
influenza	infectious disease that affects the nose and lungs
microscope	instrument with lenses for magnifying things
nutrition	process for providing food for your body
outpatient	referring to a sick person who is treated without staying in a hospital
seizures	sudden attacks of a disease that cause uncontrollable movements and result from changes in brain electrical activity
surgery	operation
symptoms	things that show you have an illness
therapist	someone trained to treat health problems with methods other than drugs or surgery
tissue	the substance an organ is made of
tumors	growths in the body that have no function
vaccinations	shots to keep a person from getting diseases
vibrate	to move back and forth very quickly
virus	microscopic organism that causes disease

For Further Information

Books

Goulding, Sylvia. *Illness and Injury*. Vero Beach, FL: Rourke Publishing, 2004.

Koellhoffer, Tara. *Health and Medicine*. New York: Chelsea Clubhouse, 2006.

Web Sites

Everyday Illnesses and Injuries
kidshealth.org/kid/ill_injure/index.html

Why is hand washing so important?
kidshealth.org/parent/general/sick/hand_washing.html

Kid's Health
www.cyh.com/HealthTopics/HealthTopicCategories.aspx?&p=285

Publisher's note to educators and parents: Our editors have carefully reviewed these Web sites to ensure that they are suitable for students. Many Web sites change frequently, however, and we cannot guarantee that a site's future contents will continue to meet our high standards of quality and educational value. Be advised that students should be closely supervised whenever they access the Internet.

Index